TELL US MORE ABOUT NATURE, GRANDPA!

Written By Ed Linz

This book is dedicated to my parents, Eddie and Clarice, who raised me with unrelenting love.

Over the years, as a parent and grandparent, I have observed a strong interest in nature in so many children. The purpose of this book is to bring together families as they read questions about the wonders of nature. I have intentionally used some vocabulary (e.g., "electron") which may be new to our younger readers; I am hoping that they will be intrigued to ask an adult, or even better, to do research on their own. A few of the topics discussed are frequently taught in middle school science classes (e.g., the composition and characteristics of light), but my intent is to introduce readers to several different basic science concepts to provide a beginning level of understanding – and, hopefully, to nurture a fascination of the world around us.

As a retired classroom science teacher, I have enjoyed considerable experience with students asking "off the wall" questions" about a wide variety of aspects of nature. My goal is to answer some of those typical questions. Several pages could be devoted to providing detailed answers, but my intent has been to provide as much interesting information as possible within space limits. I encourage readers to engage in further discussion and research on these and other aspects of nature.

Parenting and grandparenting are universal skills. Because different cultures use different terms to address each other, I have sprinkled that usage throughout these stories. On the following page there is a table showing some of the words in different cultures used for grandparent and grandmother.

I continue to be grateful to fellow parents and grandparents who assisted in the development of this book, especially Bruce and Mary Jane Heater, Chip and Mary Seymour, Lynn Mulholland, Bob and Peggy Joy Sullivan, Rose Bannister, and my long-time concept guru and agent, Aaron Spurway.

TABLE OF CONTENTS

FAMILY TERMS USED IN DIFFERENT CULTURES

(Not intended to be inclusive)

(in many cultures, terms are different for
maternal or paternal grandparents)

Some Typical American Terms	Grandfather PopPop Grandpa Grampa Gramps Grandad	Grandmother Grandma Nana Granny Gram Grammie	Several ethnicities use different terms for Father's and Mother's parents
Culture			
Indian (Hindi)	Nana DaaDaa Jii	Nani DaaDee Jii	
Korean	Harabeoji Jobu Oejubu	Halmeoni Jomo Oejomo	Father's parents Mother's parents
Swahili	Babu	Bibi	
Hebrew	Saba Zayda	Savta Bubbe	
Hispanic	Abuelo	Abuela Abbi	
Japanese	Ojiisan Sofu	Obaasan Sobo	Informal terms
German	Grosvater	Grosmutter	
Chinese	Ye ye Wai gong	Nai nai Wai po	Father's parents Mother's parents

GRAMPA, WHY DON'T LIGHTNING AND THUNDER HAPPEN AT THE SAME TIME?

EMILY, ACTUALLY THEY DO OCCUR at the same time. Lightning happens because electrical charges build up in clouds due to rapid air movement, like in a thunderstorm. When large numbers of opposite charges (they are called positive and negative) are present in other clouds or on the surface of the earth, an intense attraction occurs between the positive and negative which creates a large release of energy, almost instantaneously. This release is seen because this enormous amount of energy heats the air around the movement of these charges to over 50,000 degrees Fahrenheit. This creates a very bright flash which we call lightning. At the same time, this heated air races away at such high speed that it creates a shock wave we hear as a loud sound, which we call thunder.

We see the lightning almost instantly because light travels at nearly 200,000 miles per second, but the sound from the thunder moves much slower in air – about one mile in 5 seconds. You can use these facts to estimate how far away the lightning took place. When you see lightning, start counting the seconds until you hear the thunder. Divide that number by 5 and that is about how far away the lightning took place. For example, if you count to ten, the lightning was about 2 miles away.

Most lightning strikes (about 80%) never reach Earth but go from cloud to cloud. You may think that lightning occurs only in thunderstorms, but it can also take place during volcanic eruptions, forest fires, tornadoes, and even snow storms (called thundersnow).

JOBU, THIS SUMMER I KEEP HEARING ABOUT A HEAT DOME...WHAT IS THAT?

I T'S ALSO A NEW TERM to me, Byung-Ho. Ever since I came to this country 65 years ago, we have called a streak of hot weather a "heat wave." Sometimes this would last a week, or even several weeks during the summer, but we when we were inside, we just sat in front of a fan to cool off. When outside, we suffered.

This new (to me) term, Heat Dome, is simply meteorologists' latest way of explaining a weather phenomenon where high air pressure settles over a large region trapping hot air under it for an extended period. A good way of looking at it is to think of your mom putting a lid on a skillet that is set on high while cooking your dinner. The energy being generated by the stove heats the skillet and everything inside it. But with the lid on top, there is no easy way for the heat in the skillet to escape....so the temperature inside the skillet gets hotter.

Heat domes are of varying durations. Some last only a few days, but others have been known to extend for several weeks. We just have to wait until a new weather pattern emerges to cause the high pressure area to start to move – like taking the lid off that skillet.

You can blame it all on the sun. Its rays heat Earth in uneven patterns creating temperature differences in air. This means that cooler air shrinks in size, allowing surrounding air to come into that area. More air, more weight, more pressure below. That's where the high pressure comes from, and sometimes a heat dome is formed. Thank goodness for A/C !

GRANDFATHER, WHY DO DIFFERENT TREES HAVE DIFFERENT COLORS IN FALL?

W ELL, CAMILA, FIRST OF ALL, not all trees change colors in Fall. Only "deciduous" trees change colors and drop their leaves. The word deciduous means "falling off or shedding annually." Evergreen trees stay green all year and are called "coniferous."

During spring and summer leaves on deciduous trees are green due to large amounts of chlorophyll in the leaves which absorb sunlight in a process called "photosynthesis." This converts sunlight energy into sugars which feed the tree.

As the amount of daylight becomes less in Fall, temperatures decrease causing chlorophyll to break down and disappear. This allows yellow and red colors already in the leaves to be seen. Some trees such as oaks and dogwoods have even darker red leaves due to chemical changes. Sugars trapped in these leaves generate new colors that were not present earlier in the year.

By the end of summer, leaves self-destruct to protect the tree from the cold ahead. A layer of cells where the leaf is attached to the tree branch begins to stop water flow into and out of the leaf causing it to dry up and detach, especially when the wind blows. The bare tree is now prepared to battle winter!

POPPA, I KNOW THAT WATER IS HEAVY, SO HOW CAN IT STAY UP IN CLOUDS WITHOUT FALLING UNTIL IT RAINS?

W ATER IS HEAVY, JULIA.....YOU KNOW that from carrying a watering can for our garden. And there is water in every cloud. Since it is far heavier than air, you would be correct to assume that it cannot stay in a cloud. The average cumulus cloud full of water weighs over a million pounds but that water stays there.

However, there are other factors. The water gathered in the cloud is due to warm, humid air rising. As this air goes higher and higher, it enters cooler and cooler temperatures causing this vapor to condense into tiny water droplets. These very tiny water molecules in the clouds are definitely trying to fall, but rising air currents inside the clouds are trying to blow them upwards. A point is quickly reached where the force of gravity trying to push the water droplets downward is balanced by the wind force pushing them upwards. This collection of water droplets is now visible to us below as white, puffy floating objects which we call clouds.

Also, air itself has weight. At sea level, a square inch of the air above us weighs close to 15 pounds. The moist air in the clouds is lighter than the dry air below it, causing the cloud to "float" in the sky while the cloud grows in size.

If there is enough moist air rising to make these water droplets larger, they finally have enough weight to exceed the force of air holding them up, and they begin to fall as rain. If it is cold enough in the cloud, the droplets may freeze and turn into hail. Snowflakes are just ice crystals falling from clouds.

WHY DO TORNADOES OCCUR SO OFTEN IN SOME PLACES, GRANDPA, BUT NOT IN OTHERS?

FIRST OF ALL, SAM, YOU have to understand how tornadoes are formed. They begin inside a thunderstorm where warm, moist air collides with cold, dry air. The warm air rises, sometimes in a spinning motion due to winds inside the cloud moving in different directions at different speeds. If this spinning turns upward, the weight due to rain and hail inside causes this section to start falling slowly out of the cloud. From the ground, this part of the cloud looks like a dark funnel. The gravitational attraction with Earth will cause the funnel to suddenly connect to ground. Once it touches, the high swirling winds (sometimes over 300 mph) create incredible damage. Sometimes severe damage occurs next to areas with no destruction. Meteorologists use a scale ranging from 0 to 5 to evaluate the amount of damage done by a tornado.

If the funnel touches water, it's called a "waterspout." One of the strangest facts about tornadoes is that they sometimes lift up from the ground and then touch down again miles away. There are no good answers yet as to why this happens.

Here in the U.S. moist air moving north from the Gulf of America (previously known as the Gulf of Mexico) collides with cooler air from Canada over the central part of the U.S. between the Rocky Mountains in the west and the Appalachian Mountains in the east, usually during the spring and early summer. Although it isn't an official term, this region is often called "Tornado Alley." Tornadoes also occur frequently in Florida, but in most other states, far less often.

POPPOP, SOME BOY AT SCHOOL CLAIMS THAT HE SAW A GREEN FLASH AT SUNSET WHILE HE WAS ON VACATION IN HAWAII. DID HE MAKE THIS UP OR WAS IT REAL?

A green flash above a setting sun

A glass prism separating white light into colors

I HAVE NO WAY OF KNOWING, Clarice, if that young fellow actually saw something green at sunset or not. A lot of folks go to beaches to watch sunsets hoping to see a brief flash of green light as the sun sets, but most are disappointed when they see no such thing.

But there really is such an event as a "green flash" during <u>some</u> sunsets. It's rarely seen because you have to have unique atmospheric conditions which cause different colors of light to bend in different amounts. This bending of light is called "refraction" and happens due to different wavelengths of light bending at different angles as they enter a denser or less dense substance (called a medium).

I think that you have probably seen in your science classes at school how a glass prism creates an array of colors when white light passes through it. Light from the sun is made up of different wavelengths and energy and each bends a different amount as it passes at an angle through different densities of the atmosphere above Earth. Red is bent the least and this is why we often see a reddish sky at sunset. Violet and blue are bent more and tend to weaken quickly leaving green, yellow, orange and red. Sometimes, not that often, there will be a very brief flash of green which appears just above the setting sun before the yellow-reddish colors dominate. Because it is visible for such a short period of time, it is called "the green flash." This fascinating scene takes place only at sunrise or sunset when the sun enters our local atmosphere at a sharp angle; it can't happen when the sun is overhead during the day.

GRANDDAD, WHEN WE GO TO THE OCEAN, WE SEE BOTH HIGH AND LOW TIDES EVERY DAY. WHAT CAUSES THIS?

Same scene at high tide..........in between..........low tide

GINGER, TIDES ARE DUE TO the mysterious force of gravity. I say "mysterious," because all we know is that there is a force of attraction between any two objects based on their mass and how far apart they are. We don't know why. It's a mystery!!!

Because the Sun, Moon and Earth all have very large masses, they are continually attracted to each other, even though there are incredibly large distances separating them. The moon never crashes into Earth because the moon is moving so fast. As it is pulled 10 meters (m) toward Earth, it has moved so fast in a straight line away from Earth it would be 10 m away if it were not falling toward Earth. So it stays the same distance from Earth – even though it is falling! The same happens to Earth as we travel around the sun. As long as everything keeps moving at high speeds, everything stays in place, and we are safe.

As the moon passes over a section of ocean, the gravitational force pulls seawater up towards it...this is "high" tide. The sun has the same effect on the ocean, but it's a lesser one because it is so much further from Earth. This water "bulge" also occurs on the side of Earth farthest from the moon. It's complicated, but ALL of Earth is being pulled towards the moon, so the land mass in the center of Earth is being pulled from under the water on the other side causing a high tide there. The water being pulled has to come from somewhere, so in those locations there are "low" tides. This happens twice a day. The height of tides varies by location due to several factors, such as the bottom of the ocean as it approaches shore. Lakes, and even land, also have daily tides, but they are too small for us to see.

WAI GONG, WHAT ARE THESE WEIRD-LOOKING INSECTS WITH LONG TAILS THAT SEEM TO BE ALL OVER THE PLACE THIS SUMMER?

MAYFLIES!! THEY MAY LOOK "WEIRD" to you, Feixia, but to other mayflies, they look just fine. Those two in the bottom photo certainly have a strong attraction because they are mating. The female will soon lay anywhere from 50 to 10,000 eggs in water, often a lake or stream, depending on which of the 3000 mayfly species she is. These eggs will hatch in about two weeks creating a waterborne version of the mayfly called a nymph.

Life as a nymph can last as briefly as a few weeks or longer than a year. During this phase they shed their exoskeleton as many as 50 times; this is called "molting." Once the nymph is fully grown, its skin splits open and a winged form of the mayfly emerges, called a "subimago." It immediately flies from the water to find a safe place ashore to rest up for its final change to the mayfly you see. This takes place quickly, even overnight.

The mayfly now prepares for the last step in its life cycle by molting one more time to the version which you have probably seen with translucent wings and two tails. This version is called an "imago", but it doesn't last long. Both male and female mayflies immediately start searching for a mate, often with the males doing an exotic airborne mating dance over water to entice females. Once mating occurs, both the male and female quickly die within a day or two. Sometimes the eggs hatch as the female is floating on the surface of water as she is dying!

Mayflies are truly nature's fast food – <u>everything</u> enjoys eating them, including birds, bats, and dragonflies during the mayfly's winged stage, and fish, frogs, and snakes during water stages.

GROSVATER, WHAT IS THE DIFFERENCE BETWEEN A COMET AND AN ASTEROID?

Comet Encke 2.3 million miles from planet Mercury, November 11, 2013

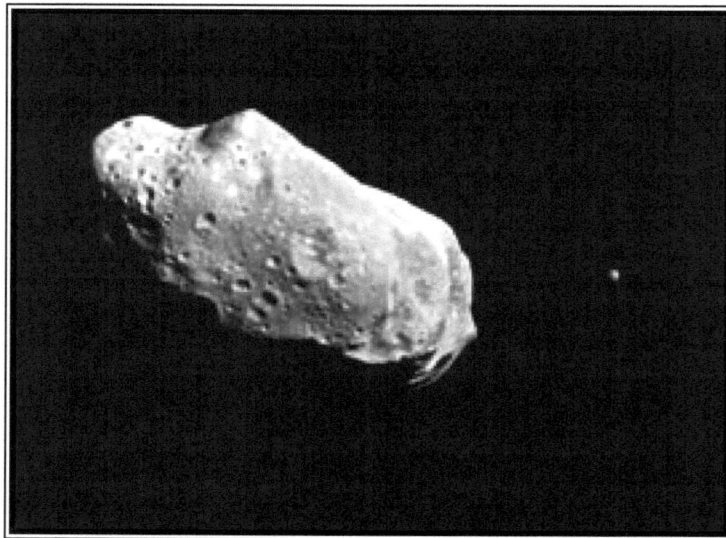

Asteroid Ida and its moon, Dactyl, (tiny white dot to its right). Photo taken by NASA's Galileo spacecraft from a distance of 1500 miles on August 28, 1993

THEY ARE BOTH ROCKS FLYING around in space, Betty. Until recently, I would have told you that they are simply objects orbiting the sun. But recently astronomers discovered a comet from another solar system that's now in our Milky Way galaxy. They estimate that it's been traveling through space for nearly a billion years! Like all comets, it is made up of ice and dust, and as it gets closer in its orbit to the sun, the ice will begin to vaporize creating a fuzzy appearance with a tail when viewed with a telescope (or sometimes just the naked eye).

Asteroids, on the other hand, are just rocks in our solar system orbiting the sun. Most are in a ring between Mars and Jupiter – not surprisingly, this region is called "the asteroid belt." They are much smaller than planets, but larger than pebble-size objects which are called "meteoroids." When these enter Earth's atmosphere, they are called meteors. Any part of a meteor which hits the surface of Earth is called a meteorite.

Asteroids are not round shaped like planets but often have jagged edges and strange shapes. They come in all sizes; some are hundreds of miles in diameter, while others may be the size of a softball. Asteroids are mostly rock, but many contain metals such as nickel and iron. The U.S. had an unmanned spacecraft, named Shoemaker, land in 2001 on Eros, an asteroid near Earth. We've also used spacecraft to collect rocks and dust from an asteroid named Bennu. We keep a very close eye on all space objects to ensure that they're not headed to Earth. If there were a threat, we might have time to change its path. A comet or an asteroid hitting Earth would be a BIG problem.

BABU, I SAW SHARK TEETH FOR SALE ON THE INTERNET. HOW DO THEY GET THESE TEETH?

MJUKUU WANGU, NOEL, WHOEVER IS selling those sharks teeth probably found them on an ocean beach. Sharks continually lose their teeth naturally because as they're worn down or become loose, new teeth behind automatically grow forward to replace them. Sharks are underwater predators and need their teeth to survive. One shark can grow close to 50,000 teeth in its lifetime! As these teeth are lost in the sea, ocean currents bring them to shore where waves deposit them on the beach.

Shark teeth are sharp with jagged edges. They use these to tear the flesh of prey. And they have plenty! Some species have 15 rows of teeth, while others have only 2 or 3. Female sharks generally have larger teeth than males because they tend to be larger in size. These razor-sharp objects are not really teeth but consist of a bone-like substance called "dentin" which is covered in an enamel coating.

Scientists have found some shark teeth fossils which are over 400 million years old. One type of prehistoric shark, the Megalodon, had huge teeth over 7 inches long which they used to not only tear, but to crush their prey. The teeth of Great White Sharks (the ones often seen in movies) are roughly 2 inches long, and they have close to 300 in multiple rows.

I've seen many people walking along the shoreline of the Atlantic Ocean looking for shark teeth in the sand. You can even find them in Kansas because many years ago that part of our country was covered by ocean. By the way, shark teeth are not expensive – you can often buy one for a dollar!

GRAMPS, HAVE YOU EVER FELT AN EARTHQUAKE? WHAT CAUSES THEM?

Earthquake damage in Nepal 2015

Store in North Carolina following 2020 earthquake

Y ES, CHIP, I'VE EXPERIENCED SEVERAL small earthquakes, both in California and in Virginia. Each time the ground shook and pictures fell off the wall, but there was no damage to buildings.

Let's try to first understand our planet's structure. It's roughly 4000 miles from where we are standing today to the center of Earth. Here there is a solid ball of iron (called the core) reaching 800 miles upward. On top of that is what is called the outer core, a large molten mixture of liquid metals (mostly iron and nickel) stretching up for another 1400 miles. This section is what generates Earth's magnetic field. Above this is the "mantle." The lower part of the mantle is solid rock containing various metals; the upper part is a very hot liquid iron-nickel mixture. The "thin" layers on top of this are Earth's crust. Depths of the crust vary from a few miles under the deep ocean bottom to 50 miles some places under land.

Earth's outer crust is not one solid piece but is composed of huge rocky plates which are constantly sliding against each other. Occasionally there is a large sudden shift releasing great amounts of energy creating an earthquake. In California there is a region called "The San Andreas Fault." It's prone to earthquakes because large underground plates are slowly sliding against each other there. This stress periodically results in a sudden shift of Earth's crust, the ground on which we live, with large amounts of energy (called seismic waves) shaking the ground back and forth. This can cause enormous damage to buildings and roads stretching out miles from where the energy release began (called the "epicenter").

SABA, WHY DO I SOMETIMES GET SHOCKED WHEN I WALK ACROSS A CARPET AND TOUCH SOMETHING?

Ouch!!!

WHAT YOU ARE EXPERIENCING, JACOB, is a build-up of "static" electricity being converted into a sudden, quick burst of electricity flowing through you to Earth (called "ground") via an object you touch, such as a metal door handle. Let me explain.

All objects are made up of atoms which contain "charges." We call one type of charge "positive" and the other "negative." The negative charges are electrons which can move if energy is applied to them. As you walk across a carpet, your energy causes electrons on sharp points on those tiny carpet fibers to jump onto the sole of your shoes. These electrons (negative charges) immediately spread out and begin to build up all over your body. Basically, they're trapped all over the surface of your body. After you walk across the room, you have quite a lot of these charges on you making your body itself "negatively charged." You do not feel this, but the charges are there.

As your hand reaches for a metal doorknob, that large charge wants to leave so that your body can return to its natural state of not being either positively or negatively charged. Even before your hand actually touches the doorknob, those excess negative charges on your body suddenly jump through the air onto the door knob which provides a path to Earth (electrons easily flow through most metals). You feel this movement of the electrons (called a current) as a painful shock. Essentially, you have created your own "mini-lightning-strike." This process is called "grounding." You completed a circuit allowing the excess charges to flow to "ground" (Earth). This is more likely to take place on a dry, winter day.

GRANDPA, HASSANATU TOLD ME THAT SHE HEARD THERE ARE UNDERGROUND RIVERS. IS THAT EVEN POSSIBLE?

Subterranean River, Palawan, Philippines

ROSE, YOUR FRIEND, HASSANATU IS correct. There are many underground rivers throughout the world. Technically they're called "subterranean" rivers where water runs wholly or partly beneath the surface of the ground. The longest one, Sistema Sac Actun, is in Mexico, but there are several others in Europe, Puerto Rico, Vietnam, the United States, and even under the Sahara Desert in Africa!

Some of these subterranean rivers have become tourist attractions where you can pay to take a boat ride underground through a cave. One river in the Philippines has a large opening where it enters a cave and then runs underground for nearly 5 miles. Recently geologists have discovered that this river even has underground waterfalls!

Many of the caves that these underground rivers pass through are full of bats and "cave fish" that never see daylight. These fish are small and have tiny eyes which don't function, so the fish are blind. They survive because they have small organs all over their bodies which are highly sensitive to touch. These organs enable the fish to feel what they can't see and allow them to find food and avoid danger.

Underground rivers and caves were almost all formed in limestone and dolomite rock formations which have dissolved over long periods of time due to water flow. There are several of these rivers in Kentucky. Mammoth Cave has both the River Styx and Echo River. I saw both on a tour many years ago. I also saw plenty of bats there, but none of the blind fish.

GRAMPY, I READ A STORY THAT TALKED
ABOUT MANGROVES IN FLORIDA.
WHERE ARE THE WOMANGROVES?

FIRST OF ALL, TINA, YOU need to understand exactly what a mangrove is. Although it may look like a type of tree or shrub, it's just a name applied to many types of hardy vegetation which grow in coastal salt or brackish water. Mangroves tend to be found along coasts and rivers in areas near the equator. Because salt from seawater tends to collect in the "muck" surrounding mangroves over a long period of time, the water around some mangrove vegetation has nearly twice the salt concentration of seawater!

And yet these plants thrive, because they have learned to survive in salt water regions where most other plants die. They are also good at weathering storms and even hurricanes due to their extensive root structure. Look at the photo of those roots reaching down in a tangled manner to anchor the plants in what is waterlogged mud and decaying plants.

Mangrove forests have been found in over 100 countries around the world. These plants tend to grow in dense clumps which set up an unique ecosystem for a variety of marine life. I've seen crocodiles hiding in mangroves in Australia! In addition, a wide variety of birds, insects, monkeys, snakes, lizards, and countless types of fish can be found in a mangrove forest.

No one is sure where the term "mangrove" came from, but it is agreed that it has nothing to do with men (or women). The Spanish called these plants "mangle" and the Portuguese used the word "mangue." Who knows? Just don't try to walk there!

GRANDPA, HOW WERE MOUNTAINS MADE?

Mount Shasta

Appalachian Mountains

W ELL, NELLE, MOUNTAINS CAME ABOUT, and continue to come about, due to several forces in nature. What each of these forces has in common is that the energy comes from deep within Earth.

Mountains are created in several ways. The easiest to understand are those formed by volcanoes erupting molten rock (lava) from inside Earth which cools once it hits air. How dense (thick) this lava is determines whether the new mountain has a gentle slope (called a "shield volcano") or a very steep slope (a "stratovolcano"). The mountain I climbed many years ago in Africa, Kilimanjaro, was one of these stratovolcanoes. Several mountains in the U.S. - Mount Shasta, Mount Hood, and Mount Rainer - are also this type.

The immense rock plates inside Earth which float between our surface and the molten interior are called "tectonic plates." The slow movement of these plates involve collisions with each other resulting in a "something's gotta give" situation. When a collision occurs, Earth's crust tends to buckle and fold (a bulge is formed) creating what is called a "fold mountain." Mount Everest and our own Appalachian Mountains are fold mountains.

Another type of mountain is the "block" mountain. These are also created by tectonic plate motion where the pressure is so great that a block of Earth's surface is pushed up, while another drops down. Most of these mountains are flat on top (this part is called a mesa) with steep sides. The Harz Mountains in Germany and our Sierra Mountains are this type.

GRAMPS, WHAT IS THE DIFFERENCE BETWEEN BACTERIA AND A VIRUS?

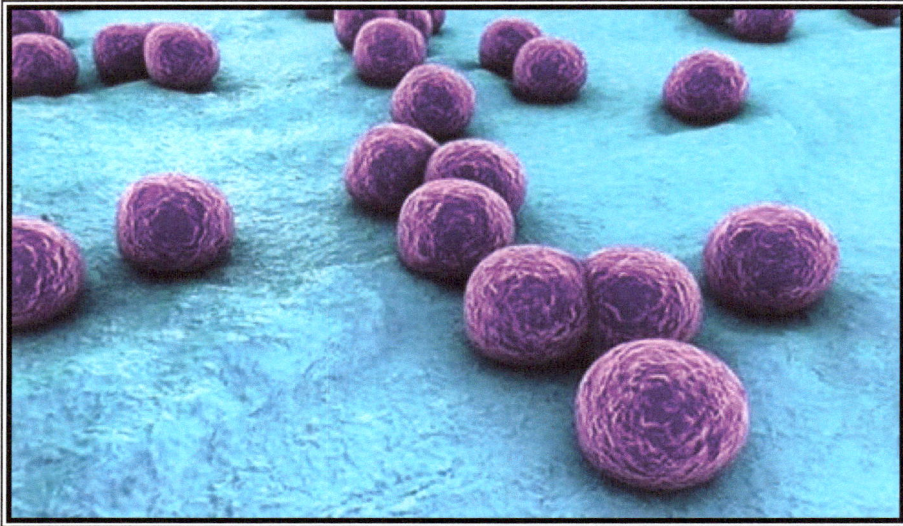

Staphylococcus Aureus Bacteria

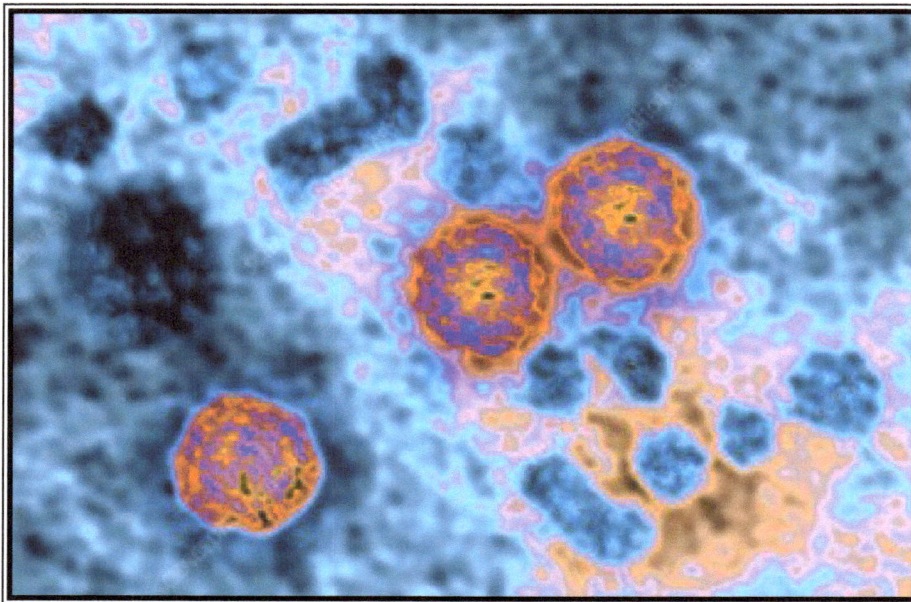

Hepatitis B Virus

W E LIVE IN A SEA of both, Ella. Viruses and bacteria are always all around us, and often inside us. Both can create serious medical problems, but they are very different.

Bacteria are living organisms that produce their own energy and can re-produce. They are everywhere – in soil, plant roots, the air around us, and in our digestive systems (where they help us digest food). Bacteria are single cells which are up to 10 times larger than viruses and can be seen through a light microscope. They reproduce by splitting into two cells. A bacterial infection is usually localized in a specific part of the body, such as in a wound or a pneumonia affecting your lungs. Some common bacterial diseases are cholera, food poisoning, and tuberculosis.

A virus, on the other hand, is considered by most scientists to be non-living and must have a host cell to re-produce. It's simply a protein coat surrounding genetic material looking for a plant or animal to be its host. They reproduce by inserting genetic material into a host genome and then rapidly produce multiple copies. Measles, mumps, COVID, shingles, and "the common cold" are typical virus diseases. Many are contagious.

A major difference is that most bacterial diseases can be cured with antibiotics, but viruses cannot. Sadly, some bacteria have evolved to the point where they're resistant to most antibiotics. The good news is that vaccines have been developed to prevent or reduce the effects of many bacterial and viral diseases. When a new virus emerges, scientists race to develop a new vaccine to help combat the disease.

GRANDFATHER, HOW CAN A TINY ACORN MAKE A HUGE OAK TREE?

MANY LARGE, LIVING THINGS COME from tiny beginnings. You're a perfect example, Suzanne. You began as a tiny egg inside your mother. It was less than 1/10 of a millimeter across; your hair is 4 times wider! And look at you now, millions of times larger.

Most seeds are also tiny compared to the plant which grows from them. Acorns are oak seeds. They vary in size, depending on the type of oak, but most are about an inch in length. The acorn has a tough outer shell to protect its interior. Eventually, with sufficient moisture and warm temperatures, the acorn swells and sends out a primary root downward. This becomes the oak's initial anchor in the ground. Next a small tender green shoot breaks through the surface above; this is called a seedling. Up to this time, all the nutrition is provided by the acorn, but once it's a seedling, it relies on food from the soil and water, along with sunlight, to allow the oak to grow.

Most acorns which fall directly under an oak do not germinate because it takes sunlight and moisture to grow a root. Small animals, such as squirrels, often help by carrying acorns to a sunny location. Oaks have slow growth cycles and don't become saplings (small trees) for another 4 to 5 years.

Oaks often live 200 years or more and can grow to great size. A famous one had a trunk which was nearly 32 feet around. The spread of its leaves in summer was close to 120 feet – about half the length of a football field. When it finally perished in a storm, it was estimated to be over 450 years old.

ABUELO, WHAT IS DIRT MADE OF?

The three types of soil

BEATRIX, THIS IS NOT A **simple question!** No two scoops of dirt are the same because each is a different mixture of "stuff." All dirt used to be rock, but most of this was long ago broken down into tiny particles. Technically, dirt is just a mixture of clay, sand, and silt (a mixture of rock dust and minerals). It won't support plant life due to its lack of nutrients. Many materials which had once been trapped in rock (silicon, aluminum, and iron are just a few) are also found in dirt.

Once living, or formerly living things, are mixed in, dirt becomes "soil." For example, I recently threw some potato peelings into our garden. As they decay, they become part of the garden soil and will help new plants to grow.

There are living organisms in soil. I'm not talking just about worms – they are simply homeowners or visitors. But as they eat food in the soil, worms leave behind droppings which add to the richness of the soil. A spoonful of soil in our backyard will contain at least 10,000 animal species and close to a billion living cells! Most of these have no name, but they are key to providing nutrition to plants trying to grow. Most soil is teeming with activity. It's always a work in progress.

Think about what happens when a leaf falls onto our garden. Various insects and mites start shredding it. Then bacteria and fungi help to further break down the remaining tiny pieces of leaf. When that leaf is small enough to dissolve in rain water, it can be taken up by plants as their food. There is actually a "soil cam" online which shows this process!

GRAMPS, WHAT'S IN SMOKE?

I T DEPENDS, CHARLIE, ON WHAT is burning. Smoke has hundreds of chemicals in it, some seen and others unseen. What's in the smoke depends on several things, such as what the burning object is made of, how much oxygen is available during the burning, and the temperature at which the burning occurs.

Most fires take place without 100 percent of the material burning. This results in smoke which consists of very small particles of solids, liquids, and gases which were not burned. Smoke can be dangerous for several reasons, especially if you have a pre-existing medical condition such as asthma. Some of the particles in smoke are so very tiny that when inhaled they can reach deep into your lungs and even enter your bloodstream.

We still use many power plants which burn oil, natural gas, or coal to produce electricity. Each of these facilities emits smoke which can contain all sorts of bad chemicals if humans (or animals) breathe them. Most power plants now have devices on their smoke stacks which keep some of the dangerous particles from reaching outside air, but none are 100 percent effective. As a child, I lived across a river from a coal-powered electric plant and found pieces of black soot (carbon particles) on the ground when the wind was blowing our direction.

Cars and trucks, if powered by gas or diesel, all emit smoky pollutants into our atmosphere – some of these are dangerous. Newer vehicles all have a device called a "catalytic converter" which helps to reduce these dangerous emissions. Basically, it is never good for you to inhale <u>any</u> form of smoke.

WHY IS THE OCEAN SALTY AND LAKES AREN'T, GRANDPA?

THERE ARE A FEW SALTY lakes, such as the Great Salt Lake in Utah, Deandre, but you're basically correct about oceans having salt water, and lakes being fresh water. In fact, the Great Salt Lake is a much higher salinity (measure of salt in water) than any ocean.

The reason that oceans are salty is that minerals and salts are continuously carried by rivers into the sea and accumulate over time because there are few ways for the salts to leave. Over time oceans tend to reach an equilibrium (neither getting more salty or less) because billions of creatures living in the oceans absorb salt into their bodies or shells. As these animals die, their shells fall to the bottom with the salt locked in. Also, wind blows sea spray onto land where the water evaporates leaving the salt wherever the spray has landed.

You may not realize that the salt concentrations in different oceans are not the same. The Atlantic Ocean is considerably saltier than the Pacific for several reasons such as differences in evaporation, how much ice is formed (ice is fresh water), and how much water and silt from rivers run into it.

Most lakes are largely fresh water because they empty into rivers. This removes almost all the salt that arrives from small streams. Lakes become salty only when there is no way for the water to leave other than by evaporation. Although rivers carry the salt away from lakes, they don't accumulate the salt themselves because they are constantly receiving freshwater from snow melting and rainfall.

POPPOP, WHY DOES THE MOON HAVE DIFFERENT SHAPES EACH NIGHT?

Waxing crescent

First quarter

Waxing gibbous

Full moon

Waning gibbous

Third quarter

Waning crescent

WHAT WE SEE OF THE **Moon here on Earth, Mary Jane, depends on its position relative to both Earth and the Sun. We see the Moon due to sunlight being reflected off it. It doesn't** cast light by itself – it's simply a large globe reflecting the Sun's rays which hit its surface. The Moon does not change shape but <u>what we see</u> changes shape nightly. These changes are called "phases of the moon."

Four of the phases have names. A "crescent" moon is when you see the least of the Moon, sort of a sliver. A "quarter" moon means that you see about half – it's called this because the Moon is about one quarter through its full cycle. When you see more than half, but less than all of the Moon, it is called a "gibbous" moon. When you can see all of the Moon, it is called a "full" moon. If you can't see the Moon on a clear night, this is referred to as a "new" moon. It's there, but we can't see it.

There is another set of descriptors for the Moon. When it's getting larger each night, it's said to be "waxing." If it has been a full moon and is now getting smaller, it's called "waning."

As the Moon moves in its orbit around Earth every 27 1/3 days, we can see different amounts of the Moon due to its position. For example, when it is directly between us and the sun, all of the Moon's half which is lit is on the opposite side and we see no reflection; this is the "new moon" that I mentioned earlier. A few nights later, the moon is in a different position, and we begin to see a sliver of the right side of the moon; this is the waxing crescent. As the moon continues its daily movement around Earth, we see more and more until we can finally see all of it, the full Moon. Then we gradually see less each night as it goes through the waning phases. If you see only the right side of the Moon, it's waxing; when you see the left, it's waning; but if you are in the Southern hemisphere, it's just the opposite.

NANA, HOW DOES A NUCLEAR POWER PLANT MAKE ELECTRICITY... AND IS IT SAFE?

North Anna Nuclear Power Station
Louisa County, Virginia
Provides electricity for nearly 500,000 homes

(photo courtesy of Michael Stuart)

ELECTRICITY, AKSHAT, IS NOTHING MORE than electrons moving in a wire to do work for us. The two main ways to make electricity are by moving a magnet around a wire, or by using sunlight to make electrons move in solar panels. The vast majority of electricity made in the world today is by the magnets and wires method. One or the other of these has to be moving around the other, and it takes energy to make this happen.

There are various methods to create this movement. For example, one way is to use some form of energy to turn a wheel containing magnets which rotate around a wire causing electrons in that wire to move. For example, water flowing over a wheel will cause it (and the magnets attached to it) to move. Other methods use energy from burning wood, coal, oil, or natural gas to boil water to create steam which then passes over blades on a wheel and its magnets to make it turn.

A nuclear power plant doesn't burn anything. Instead it uses a type of nuclear reaction, called "fission," to generate heat. When a tiny particle called a "neutron" strikes an atom of uranium under certain conditions, it splits the atom. A tremendous amount of heat is generated in this process. This heat is removed by water at very high temperature (500F) and pressure (1600 psi). The water doesn't boil because it is under such high pressure. This <u>very hot</u> water flows in pipes to another piece of equipment where its heat causes regular water at normal atmospheric pressure to boil, creating steam. From this point on, the nuclear plant works exactly the same as the ones which burn things to produce steam turning a wheel.

Nuclear plants now have a remarkably good safety record and, unlike many other methods, have no harmful emissions. Many people, unfortunately, remain frightened by nuclear power, but, in my opinion, it's a good way to make pollution-free electricity.

GLOSSARY

Atmospheric Pressure: The weight of a column of air on a square inch of Earth...measured in pounds per square inch (psi). At sea level it is 14.7 psi. At high altitudes, such as in Denver, it is only 12.5 psi because there is less air (and less weight) above it.

Clay: Soft loose earth material originating from the weathering of rocks containing certain minerals over vast amounts of time.

Condense: the action of a gas or vapor changing to a liquid.

Cumulus: A type of low-level cloud that has a puffy, cotton-like appearance.

Diameter: The longest distance from one side of a circular object to the other.

Exoskeleton: The rigid covering on the exterior of many animals, for example, the shell of an oyster.

Genome: Molecules in a body that carry the genetic information for that body.

Mass: The amount of matter in a substance. A opposed to weight, it does not change due to location. Weight is the mass multiplied by the value of gravity at a specific location.

Molting: The process in which animals shed and then replace parts of their bodies, such as horns, hair, skin, and feathers.

Muck: Plant and animal waste caused by dying or decaying material.

Nuclear fission: The splitting of a heavy atom (usually uranium) by a neutron creating smaller atoms with the release of energy.

Nuclear fusion: The process of two light elements (such as two hydrogen atoms) combining to form a heavier element such as helium with the release of a large amount of energy.

Nymph: A juvenile form of an insect which will eventually become an adult.

Photosynthesis: A process in plants where sunlight causes a plant to create its food by mixing absorbed carbon dioxide from the air with water.

Predator: In animals, one which captures and eats another (called the prey)

Refrigerant: A substance used in cooling systems. As a liquid, it absorbs heat turning it into a gas. The gas is then compressed to a high temperature to allow the heat to be removed by a fan before being cooled to begin the process over again.

Shock wave: A pressure wave created by something moving through a substance at a speed greater than the speed of sound. The sound waves cannot get out of the way of the new ones being created and bunch up to create high pressure which creates a loud boom sound when the shock wave reaches Earth.

Subterranean: Something which exists below the surface of Earth.

Wavelength: a term used to measure one part of a light wave

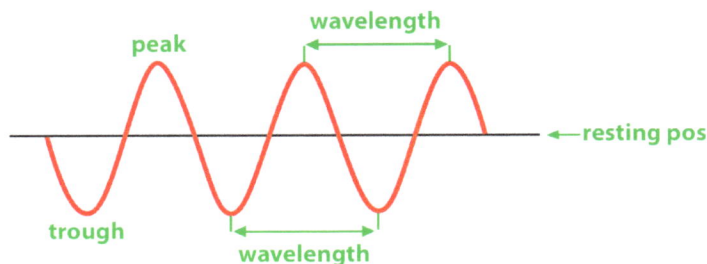

AUTHOR'S NOTE

It is my hope that the questions and answers here will have stimulated an increased interest in the world around us. As I mentioned earlier, due to space limitations, my intent has not been to provide complete explanations for each question, but to provide enough information to generate further research on these topics.

When doing online investigation, I strongly recommend going beyond Wikipedia to find other sources with unique information, or a different or unusual "take" on the topic. Although artificial intelligence (AI) is now available for researching topics, I recommend that you do not rely on this method solely, if only because it will not provide some of the more unique, or controversial sources (which may have fascinating information).

I am always looking for interesting questions about nature. If you have any that I might include in a future book, please feel free to email me at edlinz@edlinz.com

If I do include your question in a book, I assure you that I will give you credit with full attribution!

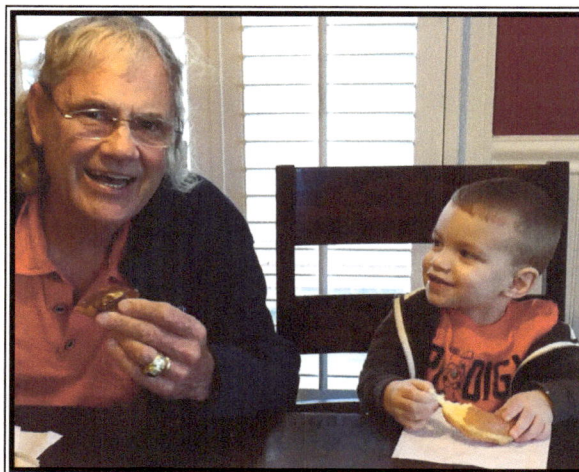

Author with grandson, Xander